My Doggie
makes me Happy

Jo Morgan

© 2023 Jo Morgan

All rights reserved.

No applicable part of this publication may be reproduced, stored in a retrieval system, or transmitted, in any form or by any means, electronic, mechanical, photocopying, or otherwise, without prior written permission from the copyright holder.

ISBN HardCover: 979-8-9897196-2-4
ISBN Ebook: 979-8-9897196-3-1

This Book Belongs To:

_____

_____

My doggie makes me happy and I don't know why.

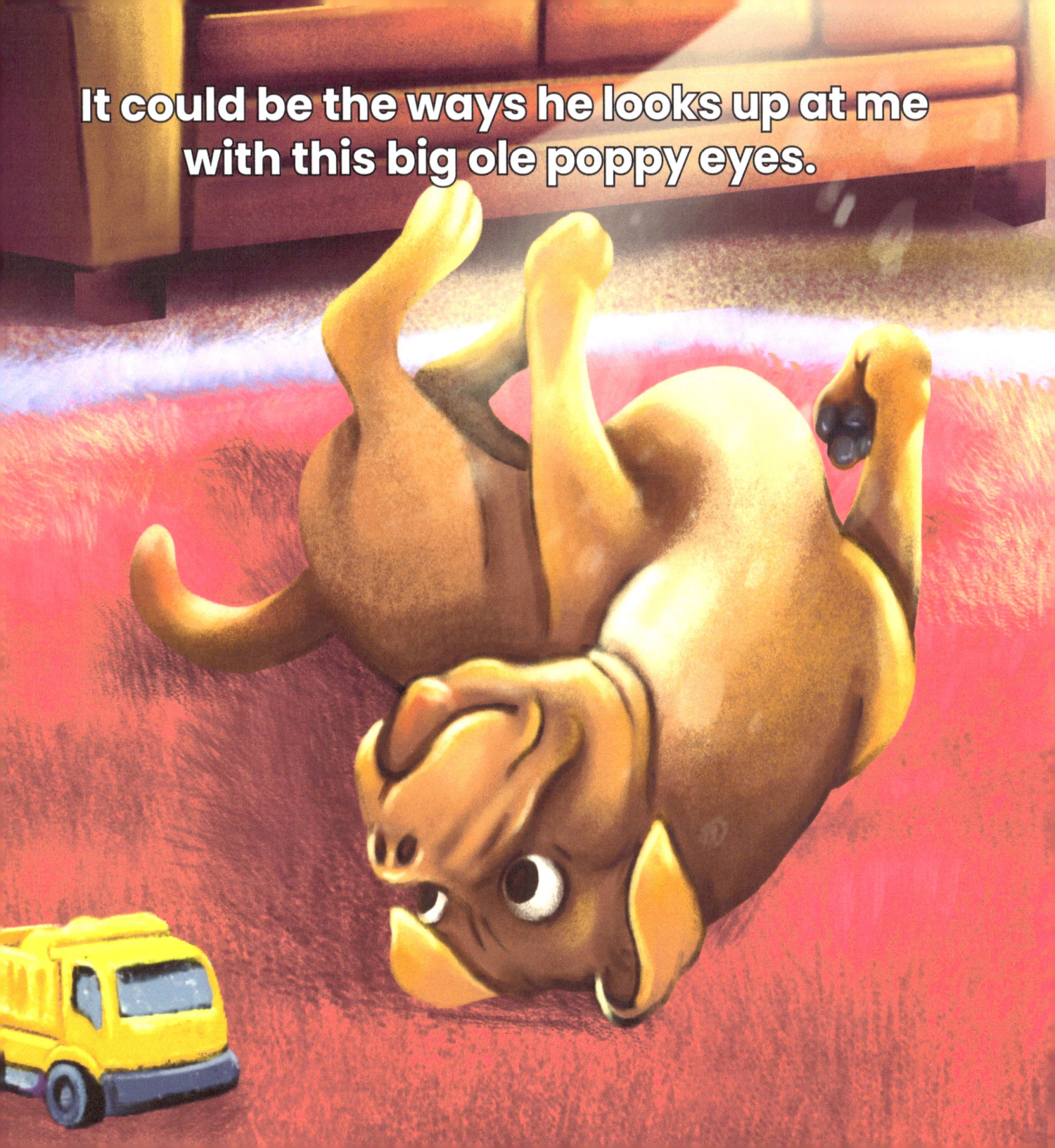

It could be the ways he looks up at me with this big ole poppy eyes.

I can huff and puff and run a mug but that always makes me laugh.

My doggie helps me eat because he knows I don't like peas.

it's bath time let's get clean.

Mom tucks us in and we snuggle tight to dream about the exciting day we had.

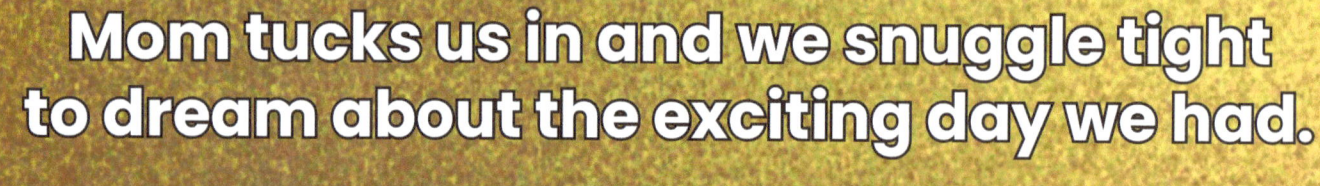

The End!

Jo Morgan/ Author

As a proud mother and grandmother and having two children with autism, I embarked on a heartfelt journey inspired by my children's autism diagnoses. Recognizing the misconceptions people have about this condition, I felt compelled to create books that offer solace to parents navigating the unique challenges, highs, and lows of raising children on the spectrum. My aim is not only to reassure parents that they're not alone but also to let these incredible kids know that their experiences are understood, cherished, and celebrated through my books. I hope to spread awareness, empathy, and the understanding that while a child with autism may have their own set of highs, lows, and everything in between, they are undeniably special and extraordinary in their own right.

www.YoursTrulyJoMorgan.com

www.ingramcontent.com/pod-product-compliance
Lightning Source LLC
LaVergne TN
LVHW070433070526
838199LV00014B/495